**FROM YOUR
HOSTESS AT THE
T&A MUSEUM**

KATHLEEN BALMA

FROM YOUR HOSTESS AT THE T&A MUSEUM

POETRY

THE **BLACK SPRING**
PRESS GROUP

First published in 2022
Eyewear Poetry, an imprint of
Eyewear Publishing Limited, The Black Spring Press Group
Grantully Road, Maida Vale, London W9,
United Kingdom

Typeset with graphic design by Edwin Smet
Cover art Getty images

ISBN 978-1-913606-88-6

BLACKSPRINGPRESSGROUP.COM

Kathleen Balma's poems have
appeared in *Best New Poets*, the
Pushcart Prize Anthology, the
*Montreal International Poetry
Prize Anthology*, and many
other publications. She works
as a programming and services
librarian at New Orleans Public
Library, where she is the founder
of Virtual Creative Writing
Workshop – a free writing group
for residents of Orleans Parish.
This is her debut collection.

TABLE OF CONTENTS

HARLEQUINADE — 9

WHAT THE TRAVELER KNOWS — 11

ABRAHAM, HONESTLY — 12

POEM ON THE VERGE OF A NERVOUS BREAKDOWN — 14

SOMEWHERE A TOWN — 15

REVELATION AT THE INVISIBLE GUN SHOW — 16

BLACK HOLE HORIZON — 17

HOMAGE TO THE TWELVE STEPS — 18

VASE — 20

SUMMER CAMP FOR SIRENS — 21

A TOUR OF POMPEII'S RED-LIGHT DISTRICT — 22

STOPPING TIME IS NOT AS USEFUL AS WE THOUGHT — 24

THE FORGIVENESS PROJECT — 25

AN AMNESIAC'S LETTER TO HERSELF — 26

GENETICALLY MODIFIED CROP CONSPIRACIES — 27

DRAMATIC DICHOTOLOGUE — 28

DOTAGE — 30

FROM YOUR HOSTESS AT THE T&A MUSEUM — 31

THE CAUSES OF CYCLONE FORMATION AREN'T WELL UNDERSTOOD — 32

ESCAPE FROM THE ABHORRENT VACUUM — 34

POEM POEM POEM POEM POEM — 35

SPAGHETTI MIDWESTERN — 37

WHAT DO GHOSTS NEED? — 38

HARLEQUINADE — 41

HIGHLIGHTS FROM AN INTERVIEW WITH THE AUTHOR — 42

SINGULARITY — 45

TEMPORARY EMPATHY — 47

SNUBBED: A MOTION-PICTURE EKPHRASIS — 49

NOTES — 89

ACKNOWLEDGEMENTS — 92

HARLEQUINADE

WHAT THE TRAVELER KNOWS

Every country is a cure for something;
every cobblestone a lozenge
for some scratchy, sore spot
in your pedestrian head; every skyline
a pointy heavenscape of exclamation marks,
cheering you on. If you are irksome and rude
in your own land, there is another
where you are witty and direct; your voice,
once a pastel whine, now an atonal woodwind
of desire. If you are hideous
in your hometown, there is a locale
where you can melt the locals
with your sunless eyes
and hold your wire-haired head high while
an effervescent flow of admirers
bubbles from the sacred streets,
winking and circling you on bikes.
You have only to find your stopping place,
find it and let it remake you from the *terra* up.
Why make amends when you can make haste?
Look there, that palace, this tower,
yonder mountain peak—it's the view
you were born to see, the perfect
finish to the shelf song of your life
so far. The end. Keep looking.
The end. Maybe tomorrow. The end.
Almost there. The end.

ABRAHAM, HONESTLY

With his own two hands, Abe Lincoln built the log cabin he was born in.

—from an American college student's history paper

THEORY 1: OUT-OF-BODY ABE

The ghostly glob of fetal Abraham sneaks out of his mother's womb at night with architecture on his budding mind. In the first few months the Lincoln bean can barely hold a toothpick, let alone a log, so he darts around his neighbor's place, plotting floor plans and examining crannies. By month two his heart's really in it. By mid-trimester he's using his tail to smooth out the mud mortar of his neighbor's house. *Mudd,* he thinks, and feels his first shiver. By month five he's chopping thick stripes of wood by the light of his prenatal halo. By month six he's strapping logs to his unborn back and floating them across miles of Kentucky airspace. By month seven he's all over the roof like a Christmas specter. By month eight his newly lit neurons are sparkling up the lawn as he flaps back and forth from womb to hearth, nesting like there's no state like home, no place like tomorrow.

THEORY 2: BORN-AGAIN ABE

When you make a house of your heart, no assembly is required, but some laying on of hands may be.

THEORY 3: AUTHORIAL ABE

Like many Abrahams before him, Lincoln enjoys limited omniscience whenever he writes speeches, treaties, bills, or commandments, and this has begun to affect his mind in arboreal ways. He often imagines what it must have been like for his Pa to construct their homestead. How many times had the teenage Lincoln built that same boxy lodge in his mind, amputating trees and sanding them to naked plainness, putting, perhaps, more care into it than his own father had? This daydream kicks in like a nervous tick when he loses things, and for every log he stacks on his imaginary abode, a windy sigh rushes through the grassy blades of his beard. Since the war began, he's been adding rooms that were never there in his youth, and the walls are getting higher, so high the house is now a tower he must climb and climb.

POEM ON THE VERGE OF A NERVOUS BREAKDOWN

—for Almodóvar

In my favorite movie a woman lights a fire in her bed
after trying all day to find her married lover,
to tell him she is pregnant. Now I know
what you're thinking: the fire is a metaphor
for passion, but that's not really what I mean.
What I mean is that I like the idea of a fire
—a *real* fire—being lit in someone's bed
who has been trying all day to find her married lover
and tell him she is pregnant, but instead
keeps finding her lover's wife, and ends up
with no lover, no bed, and no abortion.

This blazing bed comes to her
at a time in her life when a blazing bed
is the least absurd thing that could happen,
so she does what anyone would do.
She stands there coughing like an idiot,
then goes back to the kitchen.
I like to imagine in that moment of standing
that she is thinking about her bed,
wondering if it's ever been quite that hot before
and if so, when? I imagine she looks
at her sunny fire and sees herself

reflected there, as in an orange mirror,
then remembers all her really good sex
happened somewhere else. *The roof!*
she thinks, and turns for the door
just in time for the Spanish fire brigade
to burst in like flames and discover her.

SOMEWHERE A TOWN

Somewhere a town celebrates by having a giant tomato fight. They bring the tomatoes in trucks and can't wait to pummel and be pummeled. After the pummeling, they slosh down juicy streets and pose as swimmers in shallow rivers of pulp while sopping journalists snap their pictures. Somewhere else a town celebrates by running away from bulls, or by watching others run away from bulls. Somewhere else a town celebrates by racing horses around sharp-cornered streets at maximum speed. Each horse is named for a different animal, each fauna for a hoary neighborhood. One horse is a giraffe. (I know because I have a friend from the giraffe neighborhood.) One horse may also be a bull. That horse may be under the impression that he is supposed to be in another town, chasing people. Somewhere else a town celebrates by having an orange fight. This is a more solid than liquid celebration, due to the peels. Liquid celebrations do not often involve large amounts of tomatoes, bulls, horses, giraffes, oranges, or decorum, and thank goodness for that, or we might all be wandering around half limpid, wondering how to throw fruit and run from animals in a polite and professional manner. Somewhere a town of bulls celebrates by springing leaks in people.

REVELATION AT THE INVISIBLE GUN SHOW

A dapper man stands
behind empty display,

baby powder in hand.
He sprinkles the talcum;

a weapon appears to appear.
It's not like any we've ever

never seen. First sight:
the almost outline of barrel

and grip beneath drops of white.
The salesman touches the solid

nada, spreads the dust
just so, and all the gun parts start

to show (now muzzle, now clip)
—a nude, small caliber soul.

How to know if rounds
are in those spirit chambers,

haunting? All the bullets
for this unobserved piece,

to eyes untrained
in unseen things

are loud in sound
if not in hue, and piercing.

BLACK HOLE HORIZON

I'm in flux with a TV alien, the best sad thing that's happened to me all year. He's in flux with someone else, of course. They live in different macrocosms. My chances with him aren't great either, I know, but the odds of my nonfictional self bumping into his fictional one are actually much better than the odds of two universes overlapping and forming a handy little doorway, so I'm in a much better position than the long lost girlfriend. She'll keep pining away in her parallel world, wishing she had the weekly window into his life that millions enjoy, or at least an identical night sky. I'll keep polishing the glass of my flat-screen crystal ball and writing her farther and farther into the back of his mind. Until he can barely remember what her face looks like. Until she's just another dot on his bright and busy page.

HOMAGE TO THE TWELVE STEPS

1. We saw that we were flowerless through every season; our yards had become unmanageable.

2. We came to believe flower slayers such as ourselves might be poor with plants, but still handy.

3. We made a decision to turn our tills and scythes over to Todd, as we understood Todd was God in the gardening business.

4. We made a searching and tearless allium inventory of our shelves.

5. We admitted to Todd and to ourselves, over a plate of green beans, the neglected state of our lawns.

6. We were entirely ready to let Todd disprove those leaflets from his competitors.

7. We humbly asked Todd to remove our grass clippings.

8. We made a list of all flora we had harmed, became willing to make a fence for them all.

9. We made dirt our friend, weather permitting, except when to dig holes would injure moles or other rodents.

10. We continued herbal inventory, and when there was none, Todd recommended it.

11. We sought, through pear and fermentation, to improve our culinary impact with grog as we understood grog, landscaping only for knowledge of Todd's bill and the power to pay it off.

12. Having had a botanical awakening as a result of these steps, we tried every day to carry the vegetable surplus to storage and practice canning in all our spare time.

VASE

a tangible thing; a word
for a tangible thing; a place
to put other, smaller things;
a place to put other,
smaller words;
a word to put
other things in place.

SUMMER CAMP FOR SIRENS

Here we learn to deep-freeze Dreamsicles, lift bunks
at wrong angles until our spines kneel down inside our
backs, and handwrite thank-you cards with one athletic,
cursive hand while waving with the limp-wristed other.
Our camp uniforms are coveralls covered in flags. We get
a new flag for everything we learn. We even get a new
flag for learning how to earn a new flag! Holidays we don
dress uniforms (called *dressforms*) with dress flags (called
drags). Then they teach us the language of eyes, how to
ask for help, how to feign. We are taught never to talk
of this. Our organs do our talking for us. The mouth of
all pain is called the brain. This is where the miracle of
early rising blossoms, where the shopping cart turns in-
law to the artificial heart. Because cars are still the best leg
technology we have, the evening staff teach us to wheel-
walk on land. The last day they take us to a lake, where
we blare and hum at kayaks, milky bottles all around.
Then they take us straight back to camp, let us cry it out.

A TOUR OF POMPEII'S RED-LIGHT DISTRICT

A stone bed complete
with stone pillow

in an office the size
of an outhouse.

Along the top
edge of hall

(where a wall-
paper border

might go) is porn so old
we feel safe

saying "art"
and smiling.

Some men took time
to etch their praise

or customer
service complaint:

Flora gives good head!
Octavia has the clap!

No poems here—
this blunt graffiti

all that's left.
No bodies either, now,

just ghastly casts
in vast museums, or

for those who hear
through time and ash:

ghostly gasps.

STOPPING TIME IS NOT AS USEFUL AS WE THOUGHT

At first we simply wander, delighted with frozen smoke curls and uplifted forks in our favorite diner; the remarkable faces of drivers mid-crash; the way pellets of rain disappear where we walk, leaving body-shaped paths in the air. We consider travel, but the roads are littered with stilled cars and neither of us can fly. Even looting isn't as easy as we supposed: the thyme green sofa we ogle is burdensome to carry, so we choose a hearthrug with beige mountain shapes that reminds us of *Brigadoon* and the seventies. We balance the shag on our shoulders and drag two bags full of gallimaufry and farrago from that vintage garb shop down the road. The only other things we really need now are your extra-wide dress shoes, which will have to be mail-ordered post pause, and a house, which still feels remote and chimerical, like Dalí. Even good deeds are unexpectedly complex, though we eventually choose to pickpocket the fob of a petrified doctor in white coat and vest, then slip script pads in the clutch bag of a bedfast hatmaker while she freeze-weeps on an Irish "magic hanky." (Now it's a hanky. Now it's a bonnet. Now it's a hanky again.)

THE FORGIVENESS PROJECT

—after Szymborska

Under what conditions should one admit wrongdoing?
Is confessing in a dream as good as in a booth?
Who goes first?
Are there age restrictions?
Do the dead get a shot?

Who runs the project and for how long?
Are reservations and appointments a must,
or is it first come, first served?
Is there a suggestion box? A gift registry?
Will I need a witness?

When the apology part is over,
should all spilled secrets be tagged and catalogued?
Accidents, sins, mistakes, peccadilloes …
who decides what's what?
Do records remain sealed?

Do poems count as admissions of guilt? Do paintings?
Are confessional poems by victims
filed under A for *Allegations*
during pax audits and quarrel inventories?
Is the Forgiveness Librarian discrete? Is she happy?

After the project, will a pardon be a privilege,
a rite of passage, or both? Is there a prize for best entry?
Do animals participate? Do plants?
Will a new holiday mark the end of resentment?
Are "I Forgave Today" stickers at the exit?

AN AMNESIAC'S LETTER TO HERSELF

I haven't forgotten the world, only its corners. The distance from birdbath to bathtub—measured with yardsticks, cloudsticks, or fishsticks? Find out: why parasols not sunbrellas, why downpour but no downshine? Sometimes the nurses serve rhubarb to faze me. (Should I eat this or marry it?) Sometimes they bring curly bouquets. Wigs are still the only blooms I recall. The one I planted won't sprout. (So much for blue thumbs.) Yesterday I paced a ramp with closed eyes and realized I used to surf. Lately I've had urges to climb things and wave from the tops. When people stare at me I know to either kiss them or run. I no longer confuse babies with sirens. Why is tickling legal and crunching only savory when it happens in a mouth? I met a man whose face felt rough and smooth at the same time, like the orange side of an orange peel. Soon I learned this was ugly. When I wake in the morning I'm sure of where I am, then I'm not. There's a feather in the sink.

GENETICALLY MODIFIED CROP CONSPIRACIES

1

Your corn farm is a field of spies. Its ears are eavesdropping, each root a cochlear maize device implanted in high-tech soil to listen in. Crop circles are circling the station wagons, buttering themselves for battle. Your grits will not save you. Your good guys with grits will not save you. Who will save you? Who will save you from the Frankenstalks? Your hungry, of course. Your tractors. Your cows and horses, longing to eat grain. Feed them these: your homegrown corn dogs of war, your frenemies on the cob. Feed them, and know peas and hominy.

2

Smart soybeans are in league with Mexicans. They want to take over the Heartland. *Soy:* I am (not the impermanent "I am fine" but the permanent "I am from here"). Vegetarians aid the Soy-Mexican team, their larders full of tofu. «*Soy de aquí.*» Say it fast and it rhymes with *soybean*.

3

Pigs will soon be crossbred with veg, their swine bulbs buried like mandrakes. (How delicious the porkiflower! How rich the oinccoli and hamfalfa sprouts!) No, no plantimals were harmed for this salad. Picked but never pulled out by the hooves, they live to sprout again. But *think*, will you? Who might use them for food and who for torture? *This little piggy went to black ops. This little piggy flew drones. This little piggy earned five stars. This little piggy got cloned. This little piggy cried, "Hut Toop Threep Fourp, Hut!"* all the way home.

DRAMATIC DICHOTOLOGUE

It's good to be bilingual. Almost makes up
for the other bi thing about me. Not quite family, but step-

whatsit, or great doohickey twice removed
on your ex-fairy-godmother's side. Still, I'm something

like your Aunt David, and if the Queen ever dies
I'm in the line of succession. Truthfully, I prefer

circles to lines. "Circle of succession"
has a nice ring. Like Knights of the Round Table

only sexier. You may think it's hard to be sexier
than a circumference of metal-clad men, but I swear by

all the bivalves in an errant chef's paella
that my circuit is more heartthrob than King Arthur's.

So would Casanova. He'd swear on a stack of pizzas,
florins, and halos, 'cause that's how Giacomo rolls.

I can't help but epicene. Head doctors named me.
They were torn between bi- and pan-, but Pan complained.

Turns out he's not a fan, either. He'll shag
any cloven beast but me. His loss.

I've never loved by halves. The army was
pleased in Top Secret—something about my

expertise at double time and scientists always inviting me
to experiments. Yes, the bars are full of lab jockeys,

but why complain? I haven't had this much
airtime since David Bowie died and brought me

four chambers closer to the throne.

DOTAGE

Lover, let's age swap: you lunge backwards and slough off
a double decker of years. I'll slide into a sadder sack of myself

in time-lapse photography and wait. It wouldn't take
long for you not to show up. The reverse of us

doesn't work. The plus and minus of perv: *man's* perk. Could you then,
as you are nonce, touch the future me as I will want (reverb)

to be (re)touched? Pen stripling comfort to my sag and stitch,
some message in a rocket for a youer me to read?

I would like to benefit from that missive tout suite, but who am I
to peep on my elder ego? She might slap me, or worse:

pity. Or—twist in plot—she may surprise us both and not
want touch at all. She may be busy with more anile tastes,

quilting and such, collecting obliques. She may take up frottage
with a known cuckold. (Mattress ticking's the rub: better plain,

unsoiled.) A more selfishly sufficient bag may never live,
unquaked by anything but the cackle arts.

Yet, she'll be a *product* of caress. My someday skin
must bear that. So, on the svelte chance you might

want her, lover, I'd send you off to that there now
at my nower self's expense.

FROM YOUR HOSTESS AT THE T&A MUSEUM

If you will not tip me for my dance, tip me for daring to ask. Or if, having stared at me directly for the duration of a song or two, you still did not manage to see me, as you claim, tip me for what you see now: the perfect circumference of twin areolae, one torso a la Aphrodite statue, one triangle of cloth bundling *L'Origine du monde* and pointing like an arrow to the masculine earth. Do you doubt that the artist tipped *his* model? Oh, but you're right: there is that old understanding between painters and nudes. Tit for dab, so to speak. Similarly, artists and restaurateurs have sometimes exchanged a mouthful for an eye feast (dab for tidbit, slapdash for tiddlywink). Tip me, then, in calories; offer me a slice of lime split wide over the edge of a beverage. Tip me for staring back so hard it puts even *Olympia* to shame and makes her *chat noire* slink ever closer to her overlooked and under-rendered maid. Tip me, at least, for carrying so many geometrician's tools: the circle, the triangle, the rectangular bills tucked beneath such finite and measurable bikini lines. Tip me for my burlesque, crescent-shaped ass. Tip me for what you don't see: the abstract; the invisible; the squiggly outline of a model's brain matter in silhouette, negative space plastered between fleshy objects like some happy vacuum, giving form to the nothingness between us.

THE CAUSES OF CYCLONE FORMATION AREN'T WELL UNDERSTOOD

1

Yes, it's true: stunted rubes are our only fruits. They follow the yellow bric-a-brac of cornfield and orchard, look to wind vanes for brain-heart direction, then tomcat forth in sundry shades of redneck.

2

The breeze here gets so sick of us, it spits out true-green cumuli, then sets that funnel cake cloud down and spins it like a Tilt-a-Whirl all over our broke town, sprouting yard sales where none have been.

3

An oak fought bravely, but died defending its plot. Surviving it are one small girl child, dog, and aunt.

4

What I remember seeing: the twirling gale ate the middles of things, left neat rows of rooftops for blocks and blocks. (Somewhere in all this mess is my baton.)

5

To the cellar! No cellar? Down a basement! No basement?
Under stairs! No stairs? In a bathtub! No tub? Find a
ditch! No ditch? Tag: you're a witch!

6

Wizard of Oz works as a film because so few see midlands
as anything but a place for flight, and even a winged
grudge monkey has more social cachet than a farmer.

7

A weatherman is an elemental wiz. As such, he can do
nothing but try to predict what air already knows, then
instruct you to use the dead's shoes to find a way home.

ESCAPE FROM THE ABHORRENT VACUUM

What if nature is tired of being a mother,
of gendered metaphors splayed

in her honor, the suckling pigs of poetry,
obscene apple muzzles shoved snugly

under their snouts? What if she is ten kinds of trans:
transitory, transmigrant, a transplanted liver

filtering the good word from the gaff… ? What if she isn't
a *she* at all, but a beautiful bearded mountain

man, all oceanic swagger and volcanic lisp?
No remedy for identity. No one-off spring

for the inner-wintered, homoseasonal
depressed. Diagnosis: mother-obsessed.

Let's give nature a choice for once. Let him let down
his habit-bound hair, spit, grope, and swear.

Let him eat steak *and* cake. Be multi-sex
beast. Be worm. Be queen and worshipful worker

in one. A beeline made to fit. Wear it, mother. Put it on,
if only to shrug it back off, again and again and again.

POEM POEM POEM POEM POEM

There are certain white noisy things that scientists believe. When aliens contact Earth they will do it by making a tonal racket from on high. They will do this celestial honking at regular intervals. They will use the Honk Method because space can be a raucous place and science needs replication. Recurrence must blare for belief to occur.

This alien din will most likely bloom in B flat. Various branches and twigs of study now corroborate the news that B flat has juju properties. Crocodiles are tamed by it, anomalous echoes echo it, and black holes are constantly humming it. Ear anecdote:

My cousin the jazz percussionist woke one day to the opposite of deafness. His eardrums had acquired a heightened tuning in to even the smallest sounds. Tapping fingers on a table; dog nails clicking on stairs; the clink of fork against knife, plate, or tooth—auditorture. Add a high-pitched ring in B flat. This ringing never went away. Not leaving is a kind of repetition.

If my cousin ever hears the alien note, it could kill him, tame him, cure him, convert him, make him spill something hot, or drive him insane. Alternately, it could blend with the tinnitus within and go undetected. Doubly alternately, it could *be* the tinnitus. The aliens could be blaring their high-tech claxon right now, his super sensitive canals the only instruments picking it up. My cousin's ears may even have been specially selected to eavesdrop on this cosmic megatoot, which suggests that aliens have been in his apartment, which further suggests their Big Beep Machine (a.k.a., The Universe Horn) is already obsolete, unless they're using him as an instrumental test subject while speed-caroling more cacophonic worlds.

In order for us to trust any of this it must be repeated several times. Read this poem over and over until you believe.

SPAGHETTI MIDWESTERN

If the cowboy rides the film's horizon line
past the Colorado Rockies and Topeka,

he will meet the farm hand on the other side
of the Kansas montage, and plant himself askance

in a two-bit store aisle, with rows of wide brim hats
they both admire. If they trade shirt pocket jerky,

beef for venison, then play billiards in a room
with swinging doors, the pool halls of St. Louis

will be saloons in spirit, and the strip joints of
Shy Town—for one night only—true bordellos.

Wild horses from Montana will enter at
a canter. Blink: now they're mild cows in Amish

Kentuckiana. The strip pit swimming hole
is a coal country oasis on dog days. Those outlaw

bathers? Humanesque outcroppings: limestone
cowboys for a cinematic hour. John Wayne

rides on John Deere through cornfields. His quick
draws (*presto!*) softball lobs (*adagio*). The lampoon

of Tonto fades near Cahokia. He has no mound. He is
the dead the dead don't know. The bullies of high

noon take lunch break. Gunslingers sling burgers
on the range. Painted desert: paintball forest.

WHAT DO GHOSTS NEED?

A ghost needs an audience or it is pointless.
But does a ghost need a point? No.
Never mind then.

Closure, clearly, is a ghostly need.
A ghost needs a therapist.
Yes, but not a couch, for they rest floating.

A ghost needs a locus
to which it can be tethered
by an airy umbilical, but who

or what is at the other end, refusing
the quick snip? A ghost must need
an otherworldly obstetrician

or midwife. Is the psychic medium
a spirit's shrink or accoucheuse?
Neither, she's the doula.

The ghost needs a doula? Alrighty then.
Better a ghoul's doula than a hallow's evil
wet nurse. That's poltergeist stuff.

Some ghosts seem to need chains.
Some people also seem to need them.
Ghosts were once people; this makes sense.

The chain might replace the tether
in some cases, depending on whether
the role of haint is self-imposed.

To cast yourself in a shade monologue
and saturate a place with your own inner suds
is a far banshee cry from being sentenced

to limp around in a heap of invisible bling
a la Sid Vicious, neck padlocked, keyless. Sid Vicious
is definitely a ghost. He was a ghost when alive,

and a very bad one. He had no talent for it.
He was all circumstance and no pomp,
but he pulled it off. Probably lesser ghosts

hated him. Ghosts are player haters.
They need to step back, be less aura, more
trace. A ghost needs Gandhi, Twelve Steps,

or a massage of the gossamer pressure point
that leads from the power left foot
to the I-don't-give-a-damn center of the brain.

Ghost brains all have reverse Alzheimer's.
They can't forget, can't feign, can't faint
at the sight of real or ethereal blood can't pass

out can't nap through the boring bits can't
shake it off can't make light can't take
a joke can only emote, emote, emote! My God,

you ghosts, get a grip! What you need and can't get
is Mick Jagger singing "Satisfaction"
until you bleed blue luminescence from the sheer

grist of it. What you need is validation,
dear ghosts. What you need is a celestial telegram
from your mama. STOP. A ghost needs, *is,*

an S.O.S. A ghost needs Morse code
but goes with the Bat Signal.
A ghost in binary code needs one zero.

HARLEQUINADE

Low pranks make fine legends. We hear tell but do not witness
the coalminers pinning a work buddy down and shearing

half his beard and head, along with a single eyebrow.
Checkers, they call him. Or sailors who encircle

a mate's vacant bunk and tug out fistfuls of their own
loose pubes, then deck the man's sheets, re-tucking

hospital corners. (Did Seaman Peck even notice the excess
curls on his corpus come reveille?) One prank I saw,

and said nothing: Tiffy and Six poured nail polish remover
into Fantasia's mascara. More crime than lark,

they meant to teach her. Fan stole regulars, went too
far in the lap dance chair. She looked better at forty

than us teens. Worst of all, she seduced Lollipop
and prayed directly after. I mean got down

and confessed by the tub to eating tang. It was all I could do
not to laugh like a drain when the burn got in that bitch eye.

HIGHLIGHTS OF AN INTERVIEW WITH THE AUTHOR

THE AUTHOR ON THE SINGLE BISEXUAL:

> Once upon a time I realized my hand was leaning against a breast and the breast was not moving away. Then I realized it was my own breast and felt sad.

THE AUTHOR ON NAVY JARGON AND STANDING WATCH:

> The midnight shift is called *balls to two* because of how it's recorded in logs: 00:00–02:00. It is thus said that midnight is a row of testicles. It is said because of how it is written. It is written: *testicles colon testicles*.

THE AUTHOR ON HOMOPHONIC QUESTIONNAIRES:

> "Question Air"—a slogan for the anti-gravity set, or a clique of paranoid swimmers?

THE AUTHOR ON GELATIN, BREASTS, AND IMPLANTS:

> Bones with no rules, feed with no bones, boob less jelly.

THE AUTHOR ON HER BACK PAIN:

> A certain vertebrae pines for the blade of a shoulder. The Juliet shoulder I call it, for being such a weak balcony.

THE AUTHOR ON THE MOON LANDING:

Houston, it's like Earth only earthier.

THE AUTHOR ON SEASONAL HOLIDAYS:

I celebrated winter by snogging ye olde snowmen, after which they couldn't stop mouthing, *Oh!*

THE AUTHOR ON THE TINY HOUSE MOVEMENT:

Alice ate the wrong teacake and wore her home to bed.

THE AUTHOR ON WEREWOLVES:

The hairy man's revenge, world's only satellite assassin, a real dog with no real pony, a tooth parade in reverse drag.

THE AUTHOR ON DATING A WEREWOLF:

Your ass is his only moonshine.

THE AUTHOR ON PLAUSIBILITY AND MEMOIR:

There are moments from my life which don't appear to mix but are linked in the same memory strand: cleaning gun mounts the size of condos, dyeing warp threads on a loom, the moonwalk (as in MJ, not Armstrong), happy endings (as in massage, not princess).

THE AUTHOR ON EMERGENCY ROOM ETIQUETTE:

You are the greater victim here. No, you
are.

THE AUTHOR ON OBJECTIVITY AND OBJECTIFICATION:

I prefer to be based on observable facts,
such as lights, such as cameras, such as
actions.

SINGULARITY

Job was a good man, not a wise one.
So says Maimonides, Spanish Jew and philosopher.
Job was a pussy. So say the marines. *Hoo*-ah!
Job was a covert narcissist
who saw his first wife and children
as interchangeable with the new set,
and really only wanted to be admired. So says pop
psychology. Job was a loyal subject.
So says God, an overt narcissist.
Like father, like son. Or should we say, the apple
doesn't fall far. Har har. Job was so
accustomed to a life of privilege
that when the biblical shit hit the satanic fan,
he asked, "Why me?" instead of questioning
his luck when times were easy. Job was a long-sufferer,
but not for life. So said every one of his slaves.
Job was a bit of a drama queen. So says a Greek chorus
of drag queens, who would know. Sashay.
Job was lucky to be a son of Jehovah
instead of a daughter of Troy. So say
Cassandra and Briseis. Job was a snooze fest.
So say my students. Job was a cooperative learner
who did wonderfully in math and music this year
(Numbers, Psalms), but didn't reach his potential
in science, and is too often on Cloud Nine. So said
his third grade teacher. Job was a farmer,
outstanding in his field. So said Job's obituary.
Job was neither good nor evil, but a complex amalgam
of positive and negative personality traits
that emerged or not, depending on circumstances.
So say the social sciences. Job was his DNA.
Even his mullet was predetermined.

So say the Minnesota twin studies.
Job was a good provider, but not a good lover,
and he never took me to Paris, though I begged.
So said both of his wives. Job was never
an eye for an eye kind of guy.
So say the theologians. Job was better than
his author—better, too, than this one. So say I.

TEMPORARY EMPATHY

The adult human, not yet 36,
feels a spouse's hurt as keenly

as the spouse. In a few years
/ months / weeks

the couple's painshare stops.
No matter what, an alarm

goes off and one bolts up
dressed in panic.

For now they wear
a common constitution:

one nature, united.
United Nations: (deadbeat

dad at Christmas, sending
the one check per year) model

of ephemeral pity. A mammal
post-heat: sympathetic.

In heat: *stay inside or be taken.*
Only after tipping the salt

does the child see itself
in the writhing slug. The gerbil mother

sans stress feeds her young.
In medium stress she eats them.

SNUBBED

A MOTION-PICTURE EKPHRASIS

—after a documentary from Xi Zhinong

Snub-nosed monkey (genus *Rhinopithecus*), also called snub-nosed langur, any of four species of large and unusual leaf monkeys found in highland forests of central China and northern Vietnam.

—Encyclopædia Britannica

Spring in the Himalayas. A monks' valley. A tribe of pristine monkeys. Monkeys or movie stars or wingless tree seraphs. To describe them is to crow what should only be whispered:

an absence of nose, as in a skull. Lips rotund and parasol pink. You couldn't buy better lips from a surgeon. You couldn't buy worse lips from a surgeon. Venus hyperbole—the jolie laide of Darwin's catwalk—every one a Tilda Swinton, Zsa Zsa Gabor, or Brangelina.

Oh monkey, monkey, why art thou monkey?

Your true name: the Langur for cloud.

A husband is chosen and accepts

his brides. Two get pregnant. One resigns her mothering
post as soon as baby can climb on his own, makes the
aunties raise him. The other wants her son *too* much.

Prince and Pauper—to thrive they must

be each other.

Only, look how the father cares for his Pauper, cuddling
and grooming him for hours! While all around, a club of
snubbed men gathers

mating intelligence. Feeling feckless (read: fuckless), the
bachelor band won't make a move until King tells them.
Happy homes are only safe behind a curtain.

Happy homes are only safe behind a curtain. Your true name: Snow Cloud in Bloom. For now it's still spring, and boys will be monkeys. Men will be monkeys. Women, be monkeys.

Here come the monks of May, trekking with yaks—
from urban monastery to mountain hut for the season of
butter—while our snubbed Pauper, ever hungry, makes
do on sips from this teat or that. Milk scraps from pitying
mothers.

With loneliness comes trance, grit, a paws-on education. Pauper climbs and slips in turns, ventures back along a branch that, for all its solid hush, might as well be bucking bronco—he falls *that* much.

But for the occasional pitch and catch of this baby by his elders, no one helps him travel. He fends, he fails. And yet—a grand plié to his spring and stretch—he trains himself to dance. His brother

Prince is love-stuck, unadventured. Consummate guest: sharing zero, learning zip. Until the hours he's loosed to play, and when the brothers play, oh, the Jade Ballet is on!

Monks, monkeys. Yaks, tea. Yak's butter, monk ease.

Five little monkeys jumping on the bed. One fell off and broke his head. Called the doctor and the doctor said,

No more monkeys jumping on the bed!

(The doctor? Not the vet?) The curtain's raison d'être: if no one sees who keeps you

warm, none come knocking, knocking on your tree.

To monkey paradise!

Tête-à-têtes

between buds and birds: a color cacophony.

Sunbirds speak red to rhododendrons, who answer with

shades of *Yes* in blue-violet tones.

Monkey fleece

pads the nests of Scarlet Minivets: luxurious mountain
homes. (Only the best for the Minivet.)

June. Prince and Pauper have survived, travelled miles

for food with the tribe

to the land of fir trees draped

in lichen drapes.

But there's one who makes them all afraid:

The King of Bachelors.

Might women have loved His Majesty

sans cicatrices?

One scar adds mystique; two, he's ugly. And the hole that rests below his eye like a jailhouse tatt by Picasso—that one makes him ogre. Mated or not,

King doesn't care,

so long as his men are on guard, watching the trees for a single incongruous tail.

Pickety pick, lice to lip. Prince with his mama, Pauper with Pop. Prince with his mama, Pauper with none. Prince with his mama for milk on tap. Pauper tossed from aunt to aunt. Prince with his mama, Pauper aloft. Poppa's lap: best of all. Pickety pick, from lap to tree. Tree to lap, snackety snack. Prince with his mama, Pauper abroad. Prince amok, Pauper a monk.

To be always on guard duty. To keep lookout while the young romp and prance; while the mated adults finger-comb, cuddle, fuck, and nap. Misanthropy de rigueur: the life of a bach.

Memorize the landscape. Now go three miles, pause, memorize it again. Know each plant as well as every face you've ever met. Know mountains as you know forest, and the neighborhoods in that forest. Do this without words, without camera or canvas. Scan and re-scan the tree line. Make a map with your eye. Who dares lay claim to the world who cannot do this?

True name: Tree Snow.

One day King's men spot not one new tail, but hundreds

swinging toward them. They sound the alarm: *all monkeys stop, drop, and run!*

Dozens of strange Langur men now appear at a distance, many with faces scarred worse than King's. They gallop a brazen tree terpsichore, gaining even at moderate speed. Hideous frontrunners, potbellied and strong, some limbless from the elbow down. King takes quick count: his eight households

and thirty odd men are no match for a nation. These are the rules that cabobble the gods:

stop fleeing your neighbors and bow, then smile

your terrible smile. The time is only ever half

past a monkey's loss, a quarter to his squalls. As quickly as you flew before, break bread

(bamboo). Change sides!

Swing into savings with discount prices on Monkey Party Supplies! Monkey Party Supplies feature cute and playful monkeys swinging from vines.

We've gone BANANAS finding the best monkey games and decorations! Our monkeys are practically climbing out of the fun barrel!

Combine Monkey Party tableware and favors for the most adorable party around. What's a bash without a few party animals?

No battle, but a meet and greet! A snubbed soirée then
adieu:

surprise fête over, a Langur city bids farewell to a Langur
town. Members are exchanged, populations remain

constant. Rare as Noble Rhubarb, these monkeys cast
their votes for the gene pool and go,

but always with surplus célibataires. *What's a bash*

without a few party animals? Your true name:

Paw Print in Snow.

A monkey bachelor is part of a brotherhood,

living communally and devoted

to a discipline prescribed by his order.

His discipline is to watch. Watch and teach elementary.   .

Prince and Pauper have the King's eye.

While families sleep upright in a row of spoons, the brothers chassé from branch to branchlet. Each week this pas de deux ventures higher. A foot in the face, a nip on the leg, their saltation lasts until parents wake. Then Pauper forages

under the guardian gaze of the brothers' future tutors. To forage is to taste and trust

tongue more than eye. Pauper is dainty and brave, synched with his senses. (Nibble, wait. Gorge on what doesn't bring malady, ague.)

Other days the brothers' play keeps everyone awake,

so when boys follow men to farther treescapes,

no one complains.

The Order of Bachelors: a school of travel and mimesis. *Go, monkey. See, monkey. Do.*

Oh snubbed baby. Cumulonimbus puff of fur with pointed leaves for ears and rosé lips! Starless, whiteless, deep space eyes. Happy homes are multi-mothered, fathered, curtained, rainless. Your first monsoon is here. Snuggle in. Weather it.

Sing late summer. Pull back the portière on these river-canyoned, rain-fed peaks:

Mounds of moss cushion rocks: virid pillows arranged like miniature mountains—a nod to pinnacles around them.

A cobra lily poses: hood spread, tongue extended from gaping head.

Pink pendant blooms

hang in clusters on festoons. From a distance they are feathers; closer, toy lanterns with metallic, roseate chords.

Blue succulents bear yellow coiffures.

The maroon phallus of a tragically inedible *Rheum:* impossible erection in midair. Lonely yet proud.

A valley in bloom means food: fruit, berries, beetles à gogo. Last-minute monkey feasting! All the world's a salad.

The deeper you go, the higher you fly. The higher you fly, the deeper you go. Everybody's got something to hide except babies and monkeys.

September. Season of curd, season of cheese. Rounds of it. Orange leaves. Monks pack up, peregrinate

to the lamasery, humming Major Lance. Monkeys mind monkey business, baby monkeys on their backs. Cold already, too cold to dance. Now showing:

Frozen Plateau, starring antelope, yak, and wild ass.

First snow!

Second snow.

Third snow.

Might-as-Well-Be-Forever snow.

Hunger snow. Thirst snow.

Roof snow. Floor snow.

Not-Quite-a-Curtain snow.

Your snow. My snow. His snow. Her snow.

Lichen with a side of snow.

Family snow. Bach snow.

Prince snow. Pauper snow.

Poppa snow. Mama snow. Auntie snow. Brother snow.

King snow.

Scream snow.

Fight snow. Teeth snow. Baches-on-the-Prowl snow. King-Leads-the-Pack snow. Pop's-Falling-Down snow. Pop's-on-the-Ground snow. Dead snow.

Dead snow.

Bach-Gets-to-Mate snow.

Take-the-Dead's-Place snow. Ah,

cherie. Your true name:

Snow.

Your inside is out, your outside is in. Your outside is in, your inside is out. Everybody's got something to hide but the dead and the monkeys.

Pauper felt alone before. With his father's death he is isolate. And such a father! Both babes are stricken. Prince takes his milk with a cowed stare. His mother strokes his head in acute repetition. Nouvea widows

are divvying and being divvied. The bereaved ménage is large; *two* baches

can get hitched. Pauper's mother,

once present yet remiss, now exits.

The aunts, newlyweds to a foe, draw curtains against their orphan nephew. And still that snow.

How long can Pauper wander through winter, solo and slight as a wisp of mist? How keep warm? Other children spend chill months nestled in a parent huddle.

Heads bowed and touching, backs to the wind, shoulders hunched; the adults form heart-shaped havens with their bulk.

But hark! Pauper knocks! A strangers' door opens, a door made of arms. Yes,

there is room at this and *every* Langur inn. He may come and go. Somewhere miles below

a monk rings a bell.

Mama jumped up this morning. Sat on the side of the bed. She said, I'm leaving you baby. Then my Poppa fell down dead. Well, I can't make you stay if you wanna go, but it's high time, Mama, that you should know: one monkey don't stop no show. She left me at three in the morning. I got another house by four. One monkey don't stop no show. One monkey don't stop no show.

Brash monkey! Has the pity of so many

made Pauper bold enough to test his luck with a killing
king, or does freedom make him fearless? Look at him,
sidling up to his father's slayer! Of course King *owes* the
lad, but does King care

for Pauper's welfare? Unorthodox for one so infantile to
join The Order, though all boys must pass through

bachelorhood in the course of time. Whether Pauper is
naif or pert,

King abides.

March. Flowers blossom through blizzards; long lost loves appear.

Pauper's mother sits on a branch of blooms, the black and white center of a violet bouquet. He springs for her. They embrace.

A tender scene until

the light beyond yonder treetop breaks, and she is gone

again. And again he aches!

Alone on that limb with her redolence, longing to be a corsage at her waist, Pauper cries in screeching bursts.

Quick as a krait, a hulking bach leaps

straight to the baby's bough

and succors him.

King watches, sees. Why does a dead man's son follow him? No bother; a curious thing. As though this babe were collecting a strange kind of debt. Spirit rent. All April the bairn is too near, shadow and prospect, would-be apprentice, cheeky

adoptee. King selects an impossible tree.

Regard! Pauper follows

high as he can. Slips. Cries. Slips again. As determined as he is stuck. When suddenly

a stately hand

lifts Pauper up to the alpha's arboreal throne. King and Pauper survey the world.

Five butter monk teas brewing on the fire. One boiled over and now there's quatre. Four butter monk teas brewing on the fire. One boiled over and now there's trois. Three butter monk teas brewing on the fire. One boiled over and now there's deux. Two butter monk teas brewing on the fire. One boiled over and one's for you!

May. A year has passed and first birthdays, marked with cerulean poppies.

June. The many-nippled snow lotus

gives suck to honeymakers, while mindful butterflies take steps

to save their wings from mountain winds, hiking—not flying—over land.

Pauper slurps nectar from a flower, chucks petals on the ground. His erstwhile family across the way, he spies on them.

What *ails* that brother of his? Prince behaves like a giant bee has stung his bottom; he flails his head in a royal boutade, claws his mama, caterwauls.

Prince wants to nurse! Mother doesn't. She grips the varlet by his ear, gives him the look. All he needs;

Prince gives up. Turns. *Brother!*

One vault and a pounce:

they are together.

The brothers' first balletic scuffle in months: too short.

Pauper gets a bug in the eye! Blind for the nonce, he feels his way along and wobbles: a drunk old man on a tight rope.

Prince runs home with impetus. Someone new is there. Someone Pauper doesn't see yet. A sprig of a thing, half Prince's size. No wonder Prince is being weaned! Too old for milk, too green to leave—more than anything,

Prince wants to hold New Baby. *Five little monkeys jumping on the bed.* Wants it so much he won't go out to play. *One fell off and broke his head.* Almost patient, he harries, hovers near the nursling, quits his fits. *Called the doctor and the doctor said.* Until his soft mother gives in. *No more monkeys jumping on the bed!* No harm in this: big brother toting and doting on newborn sis.

A curtain of women blocks Pauper's view. His aunts from another life. Gathered around a trouble thing, faces dazed. Prince enters the circle and grabs. A mother arm knocks him back.

Pauper peers from a watching spot. What's wrong with them all?

Your true name: Nonpareil.

Your true name: Nonpareil. What's wrong with them all?
Pauper peers from a watching spot. A mother's daze takes
him aback. Her arm around a trouble thing, face slackened
in a trance. Aunts. Another life, gathered. Pauper's view:
blocks, a curtain of women. Newborn sis, newly dead.
No more monkeys jumping on the bed.

Prince's mother toting and doting on newdead sis.

No one plays.

Three days of this.

Until his soft mother

gives in,

lays her limp

parcel on some leaves. Quits her grief.

Notice: The Weaning of Prince is Postponed.

No play dates, no tantrums. Sorrow nursing.

The mourners canoodle each other and adulate. July.
Pauper—peerless, on a limb—waits.

snub *(snŭb)*

tr.v. snubbed, snub·bing, snubs
1. *To ignore or behave coldly toward; slight.*
2. *To dismiss, turn down, or frustrate the expectations of.*

n.
A deliberate slight or affront.

adj.
Unusually short: a snub nose.

Iris. Primrose. Orchid. Azalea. Prince

grooming the world's most languorous flower: his Step-Poppa.

Pauper

sleuthing Prince. Prince sidles to his Mama, angles for milk. She declines.

Weaning time again!

The tantrum this time: spectacular, a heroic conniption of Olympic leaps. His fury a fabulous show

for Pauper alone. Everyone else elects sleep.

Frailty, thy name is Prince.

Get off with you now, child. Go tussle with your tailing brother in the trees.

NOTES

Mudd [12] … alludes to Dr. Samuel Mudd, who was convicted of conspiring with John Wilkes Booth in the assassination of Abraham Lincoln. He was later pardoned by Andrew Jackson. The expression "Your name is mud" is attributed to the public disgrace that Dr. Mudd and his family were subjected to for generations after his conviction.

"Poem on the Verge of a Nervous Breakdown" [14] … takes its title from the film *Women on the Verge of a Nervous Breakdown*, directed by Pedro Almodóvar.

"Somewhere a Town" [15] … contains references to the following European festivals: the Tomatina in Buñuel, Spain; the Running of the Bulls in Pamplona, Spain; the Palio of Siena, Italy; and the Orange Battle of Ivrea, Italy.

"Black Hole Horizon" [17] … is a tribute to all seasons of "Doctor Who" in which David Tennant plays The Doctor and Billie Piper plays his companion.

"Stopping Time Is Not as Useful as We Thought" [24] … was likely influenced by childhood memories of watching *The Girl, the Gold Watch, and Everything* and *The Twilight Zone*. It was certainly influenced by more recent memories of watching *Heroes* as an adult. The author does not watch *Futurama*, but has been informed that there is also a "stopping time" episode in that series.

This little piggy [27] … is a pastiche of the children's nursery rhyme "Five Little Piggies" with common military idiom and marching cadence.

"From Your Hostess at the T& A Museum" [31] ... contains references two paintings in the Musée d'Orsay in Paris: *L'Origine du monde*, painted by Gustave Courbet in 1866, and *Olympia*, painted by Édouard Manet in 1865.

"Poem Poem Poem Poem Poem" [35] ... is informed by an episode of the radio program *Morning Edition* by Robert Krulwich entitled "Have You Heard About B Flat?" broadcast by NPR on February 16, 2007. The poem is dedicated to Chicago musician and composer, Joel Styzens, who suffers from chronic tinnitus and hyperacussis.

"Snubbed: A Motion-Picture Ekphrasis" [49] ... is a literary adaptation of *The Mystery Monkeys of Shangri-La*, a documentary from Xi Zhinong, written and edited with Mark Fletcher, and directed by Jacky Poon and Wuyuan Qi. Both the documentary and the poem make strong allusions to Mark Twain's The Prince and the Pauper. The poem also consciously employs allusions to Shakespeare, The Beastie Boys, fire safety instructions, common idioms and sayings about monkeys, and a number of songs (including children's songs), many of which are elucidated in the notes that follow.

Brangelina [51] ... refers to the actors Brad Pitt and Angelina Jolie, who were often referred to as "Brangelina" in the tabloids when they were a couple.

Five little monkeys [56] ... is the first of many uses of the popular children's counting song "Five Little Monkeys." The song dates back to at least the first half of the 20th century and is still commonly used for entertainment and early math instruction in American schools.

The deeper you go [68] ... is the first of two allusions to the Beatles song "Everybody's Got Something to Hide Except Me and My Monkey."

Major Lance [68] ... was an American R&B singer. His many hit songs in the 1960s made him a musical icon in Britain and elsewhere. He is perhaps best known for his song, "The Monkey Time."

Your inside is out [72] ... is the second of two allusions to the Beatles song "Everybody's Got Something to Hide Except Me and My Monkey."

Mama jumped up [75] ... pays homage to the song "One Monkey Don't Stop No Show," written by Charles Singleton and Rosemary McCoy.

One butter monk tea [79] ... is a pastiche of three children's songs: "Five Fat Hot Dogs Frying in the Pan," "Five Little Monkeys," and "Patty Cake." It may also contain echoes of the French children's song "Frère Jacques."

snub [86] ... definition from *The Free Dictionary*, an online reference resource.

ACKNOWLEDGEMENTS

Thank you Terese Svoboda, for choosing this book, and Hailey Leithauser for championing it.

Thank you Richard Cecil, Halley Cotton, Allison Joseph, and Maura Stanton for seeing my potential these many years.

Thank you to my faithful and exceptional readers: Sarah Colón, Rodney Jones, Heather Madden, and Justin Petropoulos.

Thank you Lucia Perillo and Jon Tribble. The world was better with both of you in it.

My gratitude, also, to the editors of the publications in which these poems first appeared:

The American Journal of Poetry: "Snubbed: A Motion-Picture Ekphrasis"
Atlanta Review: "What the Traveler Knows"
The Café Review: "The Forgiveness Project" and "From Your Hostess at the T&A Museum"
Cardinal Points: "Spaghetti Midwestern"
Cutbank: "Abraham, Honestly" and "Singularity"
decomP: "Highlights from an Interview with the Author"
Drunken Boat: "Escape from the Abhorrent Vacuum"
Dunes Review: "Genetically Modified Crop Conspiracies"
Fugue: "Stopping Time Is Not as Useful as We Thought"
Good Foot: "Vase"
The Journal: "Revelation at the Invisible Gun Show"
Mid-American Review: "An Amnesiac's Letter to Herself"
New Haven Review: "What Do Ghosts Need?"

New Orleans Review: "Harlequinade"

PMS: poemmemoirstory: "Dramatic Dichotologue"

Prelude: "Temporary Empathy"

Prick of the Spindle: "The Causes of Cyclone Formation Aren't Well Understood"

Puerto del Sol: "Somewhere a Town"

Salamander: "A Tour of Pompeii's Red-Light District

Sixth Finch: "Summer Camp for Sirens" and "Poem Poem Poem Poem Poem"

storySouth: "Poem on the Verge of a Nervous Breakdown"

Sugar House Review: "Black Hole Horizon"

Xavier Review: "Homage to the Twelve Steps"

"The Causes of Cyclone Formation Aren't Well Understood" was featured on *Coldfront* in July 2012.

"Dotage" appears in the *Montreal International Poetry Prize Global Poetry Anthology 2015.*

"From Your Hostess at the T&A Museum" was reprinted in *Pushcart Prize XXXVII.*

"What the Traveler Knows" has been anthologized in *Atlanta Review 25th Anniversary Anthology* and *Maple Leaf Rag Anniversary Anthology 2019.*